Th

Book 1:

The Elder Futhark

By Rev. Michael J Dangler

Garanus Publishing
Columbus, OH

Copyright Rev. Michael J Dangler
http://www.chronarchy.com/
© 2012

Published by Garanus Publishing
http://www.lulu.com/garanus

Three Cranes Grove, ADF
http://www.threecranes.org/

Ár nDraíocht Féin: A Druid Fellowship
http://www.adf.org/

The Magical Druid
http://www.magicaldruid.com/

Produced and distributed by

Garanus Publishing
PO Box 3264
Columbus, OH 43210

ISBN-13: 978-0615929484
ISBN-10: 0615929486

Rev. Michael J Dangler

If you like this brief introduction, you can find more of our books on our website!

http://www.magicaldruid.com/

The Very Basics of Runes

The Runes of the Elder Futhark

Rev. Michael J Dangler

The Runes of the Elder Futhark

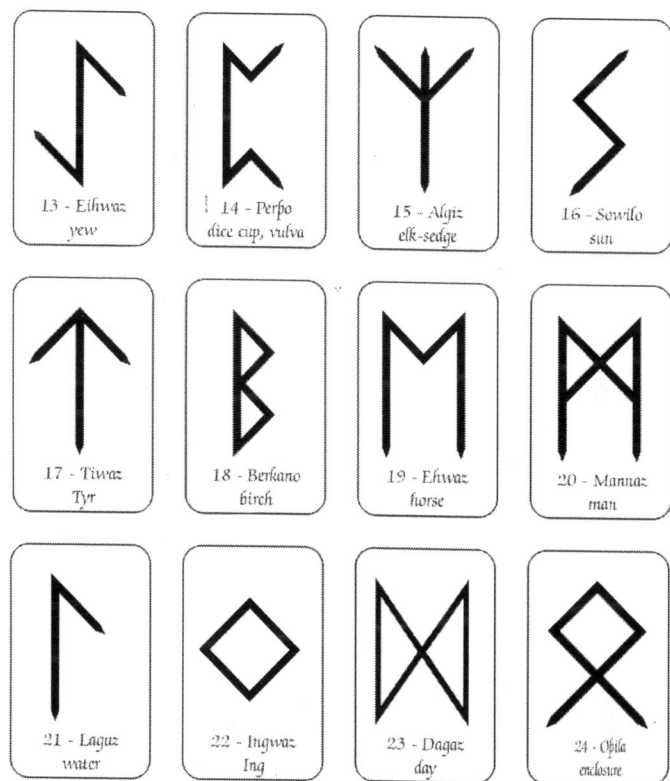

The Elder Futhark Runes
An Introduction

You hold in your hands a very, very brief introduction to the runes of the Elder Futhark, the oldest known complete set of Germanic runes.

The Runes are an alphabet, each one standing for a letter or phonetic sound. Loosely modeled (possibly) on the North Italic alphabets, each Rune also represents a complete word in one of the Germanic languages. This gives a clue to its meaning and use.

The shape of the Runes appears to come from the fact that Runic inscriptions on wood could be lost in the wood grain; because of this, no Runes have a horizontal line. The Runes themselves are said to have been given to humans by the god Oðin himself, who sacrificed himself upon the world tree in order to obtain them. The sacrifice is detailed in a poem known as the *Havamal*.

An Elder Futhark Rune Poem

Typically, we learn the runes from the original lore: from spells carved onto wooden staves or inscriptions carved onto stones. One excellent source is the rune poems of the Germanic-speaking peoples, written down by poets and monks, describing these alphabets in detail.

There is no single poem that covers all the runes in the Elder Futhark. Because of this, I have created my own rune poem for these runes. In the coming pages, you will get to know these symbols more deeply, but the poetry of the runes should always be on your mind.

The first word of each stanza is the English word that the rune represents.

An Elder Futhark Rune Poem

ᚠ

Cows, like gold,
Flow from the king;
Generous with wealth,
Avoiding the wolf.

ᚢ

Aurochs show strength,
Drive out the dross.
The cosmic cow
Brings the rains.

ᚦ

Thorns are sharp,
Painful to sit upon.
Giants bring illness,
Bad luck to women.

ᚨ

Mouth begins language,
A wise start for all.
The All-Father sets out
From the opening-place.

The Very Basics of Runes

ᚱ
Riding upon a horse,
Who carries you forth.
Worse for him than you,
But speedy for both.

ᚲ
Torch blazes in the hall
Where folk find rest;
Burning to the touch,
And dangerous for children.

ᚷ
Gifts are the responsibility
of those who have much.
Generous folk are loved
and known by all.

ᚹ
Joy comes from freedom,
Which lightens the load.
The gift of the unknown:
Not knowing brings bliss.

ᚺ
Hail is coldest of grains,
And death of serpents.
It beats the earth,
And melts into water.

ᚾ
Need gives no choice,

Hard work is its cure.
Children who learn from it
Will grow wise as they age.

I

Ice is beautiful,
A sight to behold;
It is the roof of rivers,
And a danger to cross.

ᛄ

Year is the patience,
The harvest we reap
At the end of our toils.
A blessing on the folk.

ᛇ

Yew, greenest of trees:
Upheld by deep roots
You guard the fire
And the bow bends in you.

ᛈ

Dice-cup is the piece
Bringing laughter to all:
The luck of the roll
Shows them their fate.

ᛉ

Elk-sedge, sharp-tongued:
Protected by blades,
Growing in waters

The Very Basics of Runes

At the edge of the land.

Sun, the highest hope,
That lights the land;
Victory over the ice.
Shining ray, sky shield.

↑

Tir is the north star,
Guiding the folk aright.
Truth and justice shine
Where his hand is placed.

ᛒ

Birch is the fertile one
Who grows when cut.
Branches reach skyward,
A strong crown of leaves.

M

Horses, joy of princes,
Give rest to the folk.
Prideful, beautiful,
Sacred to the gods.

Man is joy to his fellow,
But one day he may fail.
Rejoice now in each other,
For the future is unknown.

ᚠ

Water wells up from below,
Flows from the mountain,
Shines with bright gold;
Seek treasures within.

Ing came from the east,
Hero and king to all.
Over the sea he traveled,
The world comes into bloom.

ᛞ

Day is given unto us,
Rich and poor alike:
Filled with mirth and song,
A boon to the pious.

Inheritance holds fast;
The ancestors bring forth
Wealth that never dies.
Joy and peace to the folk.

The Very Basics of Runes

Reading the Runes

When doing any sort of divination work, you should always say a prayer before beginning. Here is a simple prayer you can say over your runes before you begin:

> *Speak to me, Runes:*
> *I call you from the mists,*
> *And pray that you may speak*
> *with my voice upon the winds.*

Runes are best read in relation to one another, so we will begin with a basic runic spread: a simple three-rune, "Past, Present, Future" spread. You will need an idea of what you would like to know about before you begin.

In this, we begin with the Well of Memory, the location of ancient wisdom. Speak your prayer first, and then reach into your bag while concentrating on your question.

Draw out the first rune that speaks to you, and place it before you. Look it up if you need to, and think about how it affected you in the past.

Now, we move to the Realm of Miðgard, the domain of humans. This is the location of the present world.

Draw out the first rune that speaks to you, and place it before you, above the previous rune. Look it up if you need to, and think about how this rune represents your current situation.

Now, to the High Seat, where Oðin sits and surveys all. This is where we find vision of the future state of things.

Draw out the first rune that speaks to you, and place it before you, above the previous rune. Look it up if you need to, and think about how this rune represents your current situation.

Now, look at all the runes together. Can you see a story, or a deeper meaning behind what you were asking? If you had to explain how these three runes fit together, how would you do it?

As you do the work, you will find that this final step gets easier and easier. A good rune reader will practice it for years in order to understand the runes and how they relate in any reading.

The Very Basics of Runes

A Simple Three Rune Spread

The three-rune spread is often quickly mastered, at least well enough that working with it using a book is not complicated once you become used to it. To that end, we provide a second, more complicated spread for those wishing to delve a bit deeper into runes and their lore.

This spread, a nine-rune spread called the Yggdrasil Spread (after the world tree of Norse myth, Yggdrasil) can take on the same basic qualities as a three-rune spread, but it can also be much deeper.

The three basic rune positions remain: the Well of Memory, the Realm of Miðgard, and the High Seat. These positions may retain their "past/present/future" aspects as well, but they are not required to. In the Yggdrasil Spread, however, these runes are modified (or perhaps "tempered") by other runes that can change and affect their meanings.

The Well of Memory is tempered by two other wells: the Well of Cold (the source of all rivers) and the Well of Fate (the end of all things). Here, you will find the root of your issue, and you can view these runes as explaining the general line of "how things started," "how they have been," and "how they shall be."

The Realm of Miðgard is now surrounded by two additional realms: the Realm of Giants and the Realm of Elves. You can see yourself at the center: the Miðgard rune is your current situation, the person you are today. On one side, the Realm of Giants tells you what hurts you, what you must overcome. On the other side, the Realm of Elves tells you what can free you, what you must do to overcome. You must recognize both to move from your current place.

The High Seat rune is your loftiest goal, your ultimate desire, the thing you wish to achieve. This is some aspect of the thing you work toward. On either side of it, are the realms of the gods. On one side, the Realm of the Vanir: this is the place of magic and fertility, of earthly things. The rune that appears here will help you understand how to reach within yourself for the power to achieve these things. On the other side, the Realm of the Aesir: this is the place of the bright and shining gods, and this rune will help you understand how to work with others and use the power of relationships and friendships to reach that goal.

As with the three rune spread, you will need to review the entire reading at the end, and determine how these runes interrelate. Each reading provides a story that you will need to learn and develop on your own. Again ,think about the rune spread as a story that can tell you where you need to go to reach your goal.

If your goal, the rune in the High Seat, seems strange, you may need to consider why the runes have manifested your desire in such a way. Think carefully on this: the runes have an uncanny way of telling you exactly what you needed to hear, but did not want to hear at all.

The Yggdrasil Spread
A Nine-Rune Spread

ᚠ

Fehu

Cattle; Movable Wealth, Generosity

Cows, to the ancient Indo-European peoples, were a type of wealth. Because of this, you can think about this rune as wealth that can move from place to place, much as coins do. The rune poems also speak of this rune as a rune of gold.

Gold, it is said, is the bane of those who horde it: it can cause discord among kinsmen if it is not properly distributed. Unjust kings and dragons are hoarders of gold, and the slaying of dragons and unjust kings is often an allegory for promoting the proper distribution of wealth to all.

Drawing this rune indicates wealth, but it is also a cautionary tale: wealth is not something that you hold onto, for hording wealth is the surest way to make enemies, to break the cycle of the cosmos, and to hurt those closest to you. Most deeply, it is a statement that you must give of what you have in order to enter the reciprocity that allows you to fully take part in the cosmos. If there were a rune that represented the idea of the "order of the world," it would be this one.

ᚢ

Uruz

Auroch, Drizzle; Strength, Dross

An auroch is a type of European wild cow, now long extinct. If you want to visualize it, imagine the largest cow you have ever seen, increase its size by about 1/3 to 1/2, make it completely wild, and you have a fairly accurate picture.

This rune is usually given over to the concept of strength, matching up with the auroch, a species of extinct bison that boys would fight to prove their manhood. Most often, this interpretation is primary among rune readers, thinking of it as "manly strength" (opposed to "womanly strength," see *Berkano*), but it is also "that which is undesirable," with some poems providing imagery that indicate the dross of iron, or the drizzling rain that never lets up and mildews the crops, destroying them. I have primarily worked with the concept of strength because in my experience with farming in Kansas, the mildew is less common here than the drought, and the imagery of the rune itself, with its one shoulder high, reminds me of the auroch visually. Still, this rune can only represent "strength" if you are up to the challenge it presents: those who are not ready, or who are overly confident, are unlikely to survive their first contest with the auroch.

þ

Þurisaz

Giant, Thorn; Chaotic, Brute Strength

Þ, in Germanic alphabets, indicates a sort of "th" sound; the name of this rune will often be transliterated as "Thurisaz" as a result.

Sitting on thorns is terribly uncomfortable, and this thorn is no different. Þurisaz reminds us to look before we sit down, and is an over-all negative rune. It is the tormentor of women in some poems, the giant and force of chaos that we fear and seek to avoid. As the poems say, "few men are cheerful from misfortune."

Recent interpretations, though, have seen this rune differently. Thorsson considers this the rune of Thor, while Paxson considers the giants to be basic nature spirits who are neither good nor evil, but just "chaotic." At times, interpreting this rune becomes difficult: when the gods offer it to us as blessings, what does that mean? The concept of this rune as "Thor" is an important one, because the development of this rune into this meaning comes from a lot of peoples personal gnosis. There are ways to read this rune that don't conflict with the original meaning (thorn, giant), but take off from this starting point.

Rather than think about Þurisaz as a rune of giants at some points, think of it as a rune of "brute strength" and "using your opponents strength against him." Consider this from the general character of Thor, whose strength is very much like that of a giant: in many ways, he fights fire with fire, using his brute strength to overcome their brute strength. This is one way to reconcile the modern interpretation of the rune in context, generally, but never forget to mention that we should look where we sit!

ᚨ

Ansuz

Mouth, God; Beginnings, Communication

The most common interpretation of this rune is "Oðin," and nearly every rune-reader I've met has used this interpretation almost exclusively. If reading just the Icelandic rune poem, I can see that, but I tend to think of it more in terms of the "mouth" or "estuary" that is mentioned in the other poems. As such, think of this as a rune of wisdom, not a rune of Oðin, who is himself merely one who partakes of Mimir's Well, sacrifices himself for wisdom, and is, in general, merely an obtainer of wisdom.

Also, rather than think of it entirely as something so simple as just a mouth or estuary, or even wisdom, I think about each of the poems and how they deal with this rune, and I fixate on the Norwegian poem, which informs us: "Estuary is the way of most journeys; *but a scabbard is of the sword's.*" Think about kennings you may have heard: the sword rides the sheath, and here "estuary" is the beginning point of most journeys: from each both leave. Oðin, as we know, sacrifices himself on Yggdrasil (the world tree), as well as his sacrifice to Mimir's well, and consider what they have in common: the World Tree. A primary kenning for Yggdrasil is "Oðin's steed." Thus, this rune can be seen as Yggdrasil, the font of wisdom, for as the sword issues forth from the sword's steed (the scabbard), so too does wisdom issue forth from Oðin's steed.

ᚱ

Raiðo

Journey; Horse and Rider, Partnership

In each of the rune poems, two characters appear in the stanzas surrounding Raðio: the rider, and the horse. In each, an easy journey is mentioned for the rider: the journey is described as swift and joyful. And then the focus of the poem shifts, and we are told that the journey is worse for the horse, or toil for the steed. This indicates that however our journey may go, however fluid or easy or speedy our travels might be in life, we must remember that there are those who help us along. We must not ignore their needs, nor think that we have managed all on our own. There are always those who bear us on their backs, and it is best if we remember this.

There is a line in the Norwegian rune poem about Regin forging a sword, and it seems that this line refers to the wealth Sigiurðr won when he killed Fafnir with that sword and placed the treasure on Grani's back: Grani (the horse of Sigurðr) served his master well through many trials, and when Sigurð died, he became heartsick. While we may not know what eventually happened to Grani, it seems likely that he died, heartsick from his master's death. Yet again the journey was worst for the horse.

Kenaz

Torch, Ulcer; Cheer, Pain & Death

Kenaz is a rune with two distinct meanings: in some rune poems, it means *ulcer*, while in others it means *torch*. Reconciling the two, particularly in context, is very difficult.

Many read this rune based primarily on gut-feeling (no pun intended). When the rune is drawn, they consider the question, their feelings about what they believe the rune means in context of the greater ritual or events, and finally about what interpretation they feel is most correct for this situation *right now*.

It is clear that in most circumstances, this is not a positive rune: it is the death of children, a sore that eats away at your insides, and battle that goes poorly. In some circumstances, however, it is the torch that keeps the night at bay and extends fellowship, giving hope and offering warmth.

Reading this omen is, in my opinion, entirely up to the seer and his or her take on the entire ritual or divination. You may find, though, that interpretations can either make or break the integrity of a reading, and the seer has a responsibility to read the rune correctly, whatever that means to them.

Gebo

Gift; Reciprocity

The best single word to explain this rune is "reciprocity." If Fehu is the warning against hording your wealth, Gebo is the acknowledgement that you have given freely and that you will receive just as freely, because it assumes a relationship that can only be true and right in the world: it is the rune of cosmic harmony (if that's not too fluffy to say), because when the cosmos is working properly, and you are working properly within it, you will find yourself receiving what the cosmos would generally offer you. This rune is very much about being in tune with the way the universe works.

Interestingly, the rune does not mean that you will be "well off," but rather that there is a balance: those who have much will be generous to those who have nothing. Some may never manage to give into the system, but they will always have enough to survive, while some may never receive from the system, but they will always have enough to give (and will be required to give to it in order to retain their place within the cosmos).

ᛉ

Wunjo

Joy; Bliss

Wunjo is as close as the runes come to true bliss, though the old saying of "ignorance is bliss" comes to light in the rune poems as well: those who know no suffering, sorrow, or worry experience bliss. Traditionally within Three Cranes Grove, ADF, this rune has caused a general shout of "Woohoo!" from the participants when drawn in our omens, but we do need to ensure that we're not ignoring issues with our rites: for the most part, this rune could best be described as, "good enough for a party," but certainly not "everything is right, all across the board." In fact, the desire to party might just be putting a band-aid over the issue.

Then again, it's hard to think of this rune as "bad." Like Fehu, it serves as a warning. In this case, we should be on the lookout for underlying issues, but we should consider things a success in general.

ᚺ

Hagalaz

Hail; Destruction

I am under the impression that, in today's mostly urban society, "hail" is best described as an inconvenience and a problem for insurance companies. Modern interpretations of this rune tend to have hidden positive meanings that many omen-takers strive for.

Having driven through Kansas the day after a hail storm, though, and spoken with my uncle and my grandfather before him about the damage one hailstorm can do to the crops, I am under no illusions that Hagalaz, the Norse word for "hail," is "creative change" or "like the death card of the Tarot." Simply put, hail is destruction, death, and an early winter. If hail strikes late enough in the season, it can wipe out any chance of a farmer to plant anew and salvage the harvest (though if it strikes early enough and the farmer has the means, he can replace the crops with a crop with a shorter growing season; this still means that everything invested into the first crop is simply gone).

In an agrarian society, nothing good comes of hail, and so I read this rune as purely negative. The only exceptions are in *very* rare cases where intuition directs the seer to a different interpretation; at those times one can look to the rune poems and the interpretation of the hail melting into water as a sign of new growth becoming available after such destruction..

ᚾ

Nauðiz

Need; Opression, Lessons Learned

"Need" or "constraint" are the words this rune translates to, and the rune primarily is one of absolute, abject poverty. Words associated with this rune include "grief," "oppression," "toil," and "nakedness," with a key phrase associated with this rune being from the Norwegian rune poem: "The naked freeze in the frost."

This rune speaks of work without reward, of the loss of the sole bread-winner for the family, and oppressive outside forces that you can do nothing about. It is a desperate state, one that I hope no one I know is ever in. There is a positive side, though, found in the Anglo-Saxon rune poem: here, there is an opportunity for lessons to be learned from the situation, but they must be learned early (and acted on as soon as they are discovered). This rune should always be examined immediately.

I

Isa

Ice; Beautiful and Dangerous

The discussions of Isa in the rune poems are nearly entirely kennings, and I find the general effect is much like the effect the ice had on the writers of those ancient poems: ice is beautiful to look at, but dangerous to cross.

This rune is very much like that. The ice is the roof of the waters, and a bridge across them. At the same time, the ice is lovely to gaze upon, "clear as glass and most like gems." Still, it is "destruction of the doomed" and "the blind must be led" across it. There is a definite feeling that this rune is full of deceit that lays just below the surface, just below a thin veneer of attractive and charming choices.

Centrally, this rune asks us to ensure that the choices we make are correct and full of forethought and consideration, and that we have uncovered all the hidden things that might harm us after we make our decisions.

Jera

Year; Good Harvest, Hard Work

Jera arrives in the runic alphabet in a shocking manner, being a rune that is amazingly positive so close on the heels of so many negative runes. Jera means "year," being particularly tied to the harvest, a time that is happy for everyone, where the folk have plenty, the crops have thrived throughout the year, and rich and poor alike are provided with the fruits of the earth.

This is a rune of generosity from the folk and the gods alike, and again reflects the cosmic order being aligned correctly. Here, the folk have put in their collective hard work, and they have, as a result, been blessed by the gods with a good summer and strong crops that will feed them through the next year. In many ways, this rune means more "the year ahead" than "the year behind," as a good harvest ensures that the community will get to see the next harvest.

ᛇ

Eihwaz

Yew; Ancient Lore, Helping and Hurting

The majority of rune-readers will see Eihwaz as the world tree, citing an obscure passage in the lore that indicates that the world tree is actually a yew tree instead of an ash, and indicating that this tree is called a "needle-ash". If you interpret Ansuz as associated with Yggdrasil, you may also find this interpretation lacking.

Eihwaz is primarily a rune of battle, seeing as it is the wood used for bows and that it is traditionally planted on gravesites due to its evergreen status. It is deeply tied to the ancestors, and you might interpret it as "seek ancient lore," when it comes up in a reading.

The Yew is also seen to both help and hurt at the same time: *taxus* (the scientific name for the genus of yew trees) is the root word that several brand-name cancer drugs are named after, and these drugs help the patient by attacking the patient's (cancerous) cells, both helping and hurting at once.

This fits with the rune's uncertain nature: often, more research is needed before the meanings can be worked out. This is the lesson of the tree itself, as we should always be willing to go back to our roots (much as the yew tree has deep roots, so do we) to find our answers.

ᛈ

Perþo

Dice Cup, Vulva; Joy, Uncertainty

When I read about Ralph Blum's "blank rune," I found myself saying, "Wait: there's already one in the bag!" Perþo serves the purpose of "unknown" in many runic divinations. It's not perfect: the rune poems talk about the dice-cup, or gambling, or even boasting. The word "Perþo" itself is difficult to translate, and has been alternatively offered as "dice-cup" (my own preferred translation) and "vulva." Some writers entirely refuse to translate it, or prefer to leave the translation as "questionable." Because of this, I find the best way to look at this is as "chance," and I tend to read the rune in exactly that way.

Algiz

Elk-sedge; Offensive/Defensive Balance

Usually associated with protection and war, this is a warrior's rune if there ever was one. Looking over the lore, we find this rune playing a strong part in magic in the Norse world, particularly in the Helm of Awe spells presented in the *Galadrabok*, a book of Icelandic spells. There, it is both offensive and defensive, generally supporting the statement that the best defense is a good offense.

When drawn, this rune tends to mean "protection," but it is a protection of inaccessibility and terrible retribution, somewhat opposite of Þisaz, which is protection through brute, advertised strength and constant availability. Manifesting this protection involves closing yourself off for a time and lashing out if necessary.

Sowilo

Sun; Warmth, Strength, Promise, Cycles

The sun is a representation of things that are right with the world: the sun has come out again, and it shines on our face and warms us. It destroys the ice and even on a cloudy day you can use it to navigate when at sea.

This rune is one of the joy of summer, growth, and things that never fail in their course: the sun will always rise, follow her path, and set according to her cycles. I often see this rune as one full of promise and strength, offering us warmth and joy in the days to come. It is a particularly good omen on the solar High Days.

↑

Tiwaz

Tir; Guidance, Justice, Navigation

Tiwaz is a rune that is also associated with many good things. In the Icelandic rune poem, it is associated directly with the god of justice, Tyr, referencing the oath he made to Fenrir in order to ensure that the world would not end immediately. The Anglo-Saxon rune poem calls Tiwaz the north star, unerring in its course even through the night. This combination of justice and guidance speaks strongly to me, and I love to see this rune appear in a spread.

This rune shows the right direction, and sometimes will have a connotation of a spiritual guidance that cannot be defined. Again, this rune indicates that the cosmic order is being maintained. It is a rune of justice: this rune indicates that things will be set right. . . and sometimes that is not to your advantage, unless you live your life with deep integrity.

Berkano

Birch; Strength, Flexibility, Resourcefulness

Berkano can be read in opposition go Uruz: instead of being "manly strength," this is "female strength."

This rune is about making something from nothing, being resourceful within yourself, and, indeed, being fertile and creative. The poems speak of an internal pride and reaching forth to the sky, always proud (and with good reason). It is the brightest of greens, and self-sufficient in a way that other trees simply are not.

Because this rune speaks so strongly of inner strength that manifests in the physical world in unexpected ways, it speaks strongly of feminine strength. It is a good rune to pull, and the folk will find much joy in it.

ᛖ

Ehwaz

Horse; Easy and Joyful Travel, Help

We spoke some of horses under Raiðo, and how they bear the burden of their masters, as well as how bearing that burden was great for the rider, but poor for the horse. Here, though, we find a stanza in praise of the horse that does the carrying, indicating that while the horse is indeed a tool for transport, it is not one that should be forgotten; indeed, here it is glorified (in some small way) in much the same way that individual horses are in the *Rgveda*.

This rune means travel with help, but travel that is easier for all involved that Raiðo might suggest. Perhaps "movement" is a better word than "travel," really, for there is a definite indication that the horse is comfort for those who are not at rest. Either way, the movement is more leisurely and less directed in this case than Raiðo's movement.

ᛗ

Mannaz

Man; Self, Mortality, Orlog, Kinship

Often considered the "inner magician" or "inner diviner," this rune literally means "man." I prefer not to think of Mannaz as the self (and certainly not as only males), but rather as humans in general.

On a deeper level, though, this is a rune of mortality: all men will die and be buried, and at that point even the truest of men will fail their fellows. There is a sense of resignation about this state of affairs, and there is not even a hint of attempting to keep the memory of the dead alive, which I have always found strange. This rune seems to provide warning of those things we most fear about death: being forgotten and being alone. You might see it as a call to remember those who have passed and visit them from time to time.

This rune indicates things beyond our control, things it is hopeless to struggle against. You might think of it as the rune of *orlog*, or "fate" (in an inadequate sense): it is the way of the world, an inescapable cycle of events. Despite that, the rune can be read as kinship, the power of humans together, and the determination to make a difference while we still can.

ᛚ

Laguz

Water; Change, Hidden Wealth, Flowing

Often, the watery aspect of this rune overpowers everything else: envision it as the waterfall of the Norwegian poem, overflowing the cliffs and rushing down to the earth from high above, and a glimmer of gold can be seen in the rocks behind it. There is an aspect of overflowing wealth in this rune.

This is also a rune of change as well, as water is known to be fickle and to run its course wherever it sees fit. The water is also terrifying, much as the ocean is to sailors and particularly the inexperienced, again because it is so fickle and changing on a whim. This is a good rune to pull in general, though, and it shows much promise.

Seek what lies beneath when you find this rune in your readings.

Ingwaz

Ing; Fertility, Ancestors

Many immediately feel the presence of Freyr when this rune is pulled: Ing is the name of the rune, and Ing is another name for Freyr. This rune is a rune of fertility and the honoring of ancestors.

The rune poems carry the kenning "the god of the East" when they speak of this rune, and Ing is listed in many genealogies as the progenitor of a number of royal houses.

ᛞ

Dagaz

Day; Rising Sun, New Day, Deliverance

Dagaz is a rune that draws to mind the rising sun between two mountains. This rune is a sign of bright things to come, of hope and happiness in the future. It is a rune that looks forward, never backwards, and brings the same promises to all of humankind, regardless of station.

There is also a sense of divine intervention that creates this day, so it could reasonably be described as "heaven sent," thus adding to the hope and order that is inherent in the world. This omen is particularly good at the winter solstice and the spring equinox, and might indicate the dawning of a new year at that point.

Oþila

Enclosure; Stationary Wealth, Ancestors, Completion

Many place Oþila before Dagaz, but I like the sense of completion that beginning and ending with wealth gives to the Futhark. Like Fehu, Oþila is about wealth, but that wealth is different. While Fehu is gold, livestock, and other transient wealth that can disappear quickly from either over-giving or unlucky disease or other disasters, Oþila is a kind of wealth that is passed down from generation to generation, and is thus far more stable and more definite. It is certainly "consistent prosperity."

This rune might indicate the completion of a task, being enclosed within yourself, or perhaps inheritance. Really, it is very dependent on the query and the context.

Óðinn's Eye

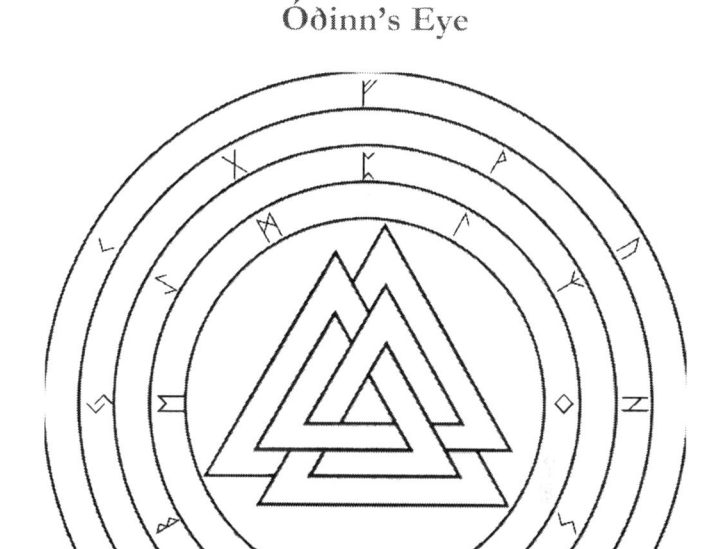

It is said that Óðin gave up his eye for the right to drink from Mimir's Well, the Well of Memory beneath the roots of the world tree itself, Yggdrasil.

The above image was inspired by an Irish piece called the Fege Find ("Finn's Window"). Around the outside, in four rows, are the runes of the elder futhark in their proper order. Imagine the Well of Memory, where all things are known, rippling out from where Óðin cast his eye into the waters. There, among the knowledge, the runes and their secrets float.

At the center, the valknut, symbol of Odin, is surrounded by the runes of the Elder Futhark. The center of the valknut can cut to allow you to gaze through the center and seek the wisdom of the runes in your mystical work.

> *I know where Oðinn's eye is hidden, Deep in the wide-famed well of Mimir*
>
> *-Voluspa*

The design is meant to resemble both the Well of Wisdom itself, and the eye that is cast into it. Gazing through the eye thus allows you to harness the wisdom Oðin won with his sacrifice, both by viewing the world through his eye and through seeing the cosmos represented by the waters themselves.

Oðin's Eye can be used to better understand the runes and their relationships, for ecstatic work, or even as a small divination board for a pendulum. The best use, though, is as a trance tool.

As you learn the runes, you may wish to meditate on them to gain a full understanding of each rune. As you do this meditation, the Eye can be held up to your eye as you gaze into a flame or a vessel of water, or even upon the rune you are meditating on itself. Play a drum or a meditation tape while you deepen your trance, and seek out the knowledge of the rune you wish to know better.

If you would like something more durable than drawing the Eye on paper, you can order wooden versions from the only source available: The Magical Druid, the author's spiritual supply and resource center specializing in hand-made and unique items. You can find the store at http://www.magicaldruid.com/, and the Odin's Eyes are in their "Divination" section, under "Runes."

Further Reading:

Interested in more books? Check out the following books, also published by The Magical Druid and Garanus Publishing:

Sunna's Journey by Nicholas Egelhoff - Follow the journey of the sun through the Norse wheel of the year! Included are rituals for the Eight High Days, daily devotionals, rites to the deities and spirits, and rites for every full moon. Nicholas Egelhoff's work sets a new standard for personal and group ritual practice through the year: it will challenge you and help you grow deeper into the relationships that truly matter to your practice. **ISBN-13:** 978-0615880242

From Private Practice to Public Ritual: Ritual Foundations I: Do you give good ritual? Each of us has a fire that burns within us, one that we feed with personal ritual. As we work at our personal altars, our inner fire burns brightly, magnifying and growing in strength, warmth, and love with each offering made and prayer spoken. The fire of our piety and devotion keeps us warm and strong in turn, deepening our lives and enhancing our spirits in the process. **ISBN-13:** 978-0615876757

The ADF Dedicant Path Through the Wheel of the Year: Designed to work in concert with the ADF Dedicant Path Handbook (free with your ADF Membership at adf.org), This is a year-long course in Druidry. **ISBN-13:** 978-1492214267

Made in the USA
Charleston, SC
06 September 2016